Live Again

Participant Guide

This Participant Guide accompanies the

Live Again 8-Session DVD-Based
Divorce Recovery Program
(ISBN 9781596366343 or 9781596366336)

with

Live Again Leader Guide
(ISBN 978159636354)

AspirePress

Torrance, California

Live Again Participant Guide
Copyright © 2013 Bristol Works
Aspire Press, a division of Rose Publishing, Inc.
4733 Torrance Blvd., #259
Torrance, California 90503 U.S.A.
Email: info@aspirepress.com
www.aspirepress.com

Healing and Wholeness Start Here!

Sign up for the Live Again emails at
www.LiveAgainDVD.com/inspirations

Sign up for the Live Again discussion group at
LiveAgain-subscribe@yahoogroups.com

Share YOUR divorce recovery journey with the Live Again Community. Send your video or your story to
your.stories@aspirepress.com

Printed in the United States

Contents

About the Host

Michelle Borquez, host of *Live Again: Wholeness After Divorce*, gives women hope and courage as they face the pain and devastation of a separation or divorce. As the spokesperson for Beth Moore's national TV special, "Living Well," Michelle Borquez knows the challenges Christian women face. In this divorce recovery program, she interviews counselors and extraordinary women who have overcome their painful divorces, highlighting steps you can take on your path to restoration and wholeness.

Michelle's books include *God Crazy, Overcoming the Seven Deadly Emotions, The YOU Plan: The Christian Woman's Guide to a Happy, Healthy Life after Divorce,* and *"The Freedom Series,"* a twelve-book series that equips hurting women to break free from their pain, finding their freedom in Christ.

Welcome to Live Again: Wholeness after Divorce

If you have this book in your hand, chances are you have experienced the devastation of a divorce: Loneliness, resentment, hopelessness, depression, anger, fear, worry, anxiety, stress—all of these feelings are things that I and the other people on this DVD series have experienced.

You are not alone. Life as you knew it may be over, but LIFE is not over. However, there is a path to wholeness and rebuilding you must walk through if you desire to "Live Again". The first steps are never easy. It takes faith to believe you can be healed and can move beyond your pain. So step beyond your fear and into the grace God offers.

When we truly know our brokenness we can accept the wholeness he offers. Change is painful. Forgiveness not easy. By placing our trust in Christ, seeking him to meet our needs, it enables us to respect ourselves and gives us hope for a future, knowing he still has a purpose for our lives.

As believers in Christ, we are made new, we are redeemed and given grace—and as a result we are able to walk in the freedom Jesus died to give us. When we truly begin to see where our value comes from, how we are made whole through our relationship in him, we begin to realize divorce does not have to define us.

So bring your brokenness to God. Surrender it completely to Him. He can and will replace your dreams and unmet expectations with new dreams and vision and will restore the years the locusts have eaten (see Joel 2:24-26).

Journey with us. In time, you can—and will—live again!

—*Michelle Borquez*

Jesus, Our Divine Healer

Divorce is just one example of the wreckage sin has caused in our lives. Divorce should not exist. However, in a world filled with violence, hurt, betrayal, and other evils, divorce is another painful reality. Because of that brokenness, Jesus came to the world. His life, death, and resurrection rescue us from ourselves and our sin. Although we are broken people, when Jesus dwells in our hearts, he creates in us a new heart and mind; he has lifted the burden of guilt and sin. We need Jesus precisely because we are broken: "It is not the healthy who need a doctor, but the sick."

Any woman who has experienced divorce knows about brokenness and the need for healing. Through her anger, desire for revenge, hurt, weaknesses, and failures, the need for Jesus' tender touch is magnified. Jesus came to heal the lame and the blind, the tax collector and the adulterer, and he also heals the brokenness that leads to divorce. Find this healing and peace in Christ:

1. God loves you and he wants to restore you to wholeness. (John 3:16, John 10:10)

2. Left on our own, we are sinful and separated from God, and we aren't able to experience his love and his plan for our life. (Romans 3:23; Romans 6:23)

3. Jesus is God's solution to our sin. Through his willing and loving sacrifice on the Cross, he paid our penalty and made it possible for us to know and experience God and experience complete forgiveness. (Romans 5:8; John 14:6)

4. We will receive forgiveness and a new life when we decide to turn our lives over to Jesus and make him our Lord. (John 1:12; Ephesians 2:8–9)

If you have decided to turn your life over to Jesus, here is a sample prayer (or use your own words):

Dear Jesus,

My life has not gone as I planned. I have failed myself and failed you. I know I have done wrong, and I need your forgiveness. Thank you for dying on the cross and paying my penalty. Thank you for forgiving me. Thank you for casting all of my sin into the depths of the ocean. Today I give you my life. I'm tired of trying to run life my way. My way leads to brokenness. Your way leads to life and wholeness. Help me to follow you from now on.

In Jesus' name, Amen.

About the Sessions

Each session is designed to last approximately sixty minutes. We realize that many of you are dealing with child care issues, so we've kept these sessions short to make the time work for you. We've also included additional pieces that you can work through on your own time (and in your group, if you have additional time), such as the Reflection Questions.

Each time you get together, you'll do/watch the following:

- **Part 1** (15–20 minutes). Michelle interviews someone who has experienced the pain of (and recovery from) divorce. You'll identify with—and very likely reexperience—many of the thoughts and emotions expressed here, and that's OK.

- **Discussion Questions** (20–25 minutes). Each session also includes four to six questions to help you process the interview and related issues as a group. Even if you choose not to share your answers with the group, write down your answers and reactions so that you can go back and reflect on what you've written during the week.

- **Part 2** (15–20 minutes). In the second half of the session, Michelle interviews counselors or experts who'll give you takeaways regarding each week's topic. Again, write down your reflections and your reactions as you watch so that you can process and act on those ideas during the week.

- **Optional: Reflection Questions**. If your group has time after the Part 2 video, discuss these follow-up questions. If you don't have time, you can do them during the week.

  No matter what you're able to do as a group, though, take time during the week to reflect and respond to each of these following items. It will make your time together much more rewarding.

- **Reflection Questions**. These questions are framed in response to the Part 2 video segment, so you've probably already started thinking them through. But spend more time on these on your own as well. You can answer these questions during group time if you have more than an hour. Or you can answer these on your own during the week.

- **Action Steps**. Each week, you'll be given a series of options, instructing you to take what you've learned in each session and make them real in your life. Some are big steps; others are baby steps. You know what you're ready for, and how God is speaking to your heart right now. Choose the option that resonates with you most. Or, if God is prompting you to do something else, do that. But use these Action Steps as a prompt for God to work in your life—wherever you're at in your journey right now.

- **Scripture Promises**. In each session, you'll hear what women who've gone through divorce have to say about their experience. You'll also hear what counselors and other experts have to say about what you're going through. But what's most important is what God has to say about where you're at, and to give you the ability to speak his truth into it. Therefore, at the end of each session we've provided several Bible passages that reinforce that week's message. Spend time during the week reflecting on them while asking God to help you to receive and live out his truth more fully.

Each session includes a Closing Prayer for your leader to use at the end of each session—and maybe even to walk you through as a group. (Again, if you don't feel like sharing this time, you can always "pass"). Take time to review this prayer during the week, as well, and make it your own.

May your time together, and the other elements we've provided here to process on your own time, help you in your new journey to *Live Again*.

Group Guidelines

This group is about discovering support and healing in the midst of this new life you're living. In order to do that well and help grow trust between you, a healthy group needs a few simple guidelines that everyone needs to follow. Here are the group guidelines:

- **Everyone agrees to make group time a priority.** We understand that family issues come up, but if there's an emergency or schedule conflict, be sure to let someone know you can't make it.

- **What's said in the group stays in the group.** Because of the nature of this group, you're going to share some personal things. The group must be a safe place to share.

- **Don't speak judgmentally, even if you strongly disagree.** Listen first, and contribute your own story and how you dealt with the situation only as needed. You don't know the whole story. And who knows? You might come away with a whole new way of seeing things.

- **Be patient with one another.** After all, you're all in process. Hurting people take a long time to change. Don't expect bad habits or attitudes to disappear overnight.

- **Everyone participates as much as they can.** It may take time to learn how to share, but as you develop a trust toward the other group members, take the chance.

Review each of these guidelines regularly. Make them a part of your group time—and part of the way you treat others in every part of your life. If there's an area in the guidelines that you struggle in, ask God's help for growth, and ask the group to help hold you accountable. Remember, you're all growing together.

Reality Check: Acceptance

In this session, we will discuss how to survive the shock and trauma of this new life—and how to get beyond the unbelief and the despair of what we are facing to find acceptance and hope.

> *Delight yourself also in the Lord, and He shall give you the desires of your heart.*
> —Psalm 37:4

There are few things in life more devastating and earth shattering than going through a divorce. Some women knew it was coming, but for others they felt like a train out of nowhere hit them head-on. . . . The reality of a divorce is both overwhelming and unimaginable. It's so hard to process the idea you are no longer married.

—Michelle Borquez

$\mathcal{P}$art 1 $\mathcal{V}$ideo (25 min.)

Singer and actress Bonnie Keen shares her story of learning to accept herself and her circumstances.

$\mathcal{D}$iscussion $\mathcal{Q}$uestions

Write down, and—as you're willing—share your answers to the following questions:

1. What makes it so tough to accept the reality that you're no longer married? How does it feel, in Bonnie's words, "like a coffin that never closes"?

2. In what ways is your life different now?

3. What has been the most painful adjustment for you so far? Did you see it coming, or was it, as Bonnie puts it, a "sucker punch"?

4. What do you believe God has been teaching you in the midst of this—or has God seemed absent? Explain your answer.

5. What do you think your next steps are, at this point in your journey?

"*Imagine* yourself as a living house. God comes in to rebuild that house. At first, perhaps, you can understand what He is doing. He is getting the drains right and stopping the leaks in the roof and so on; you knew that those jobs needed doing and so you are not surprised. But presently He starts knocking the house about in a way that hurts abominably and does not seem to make any sense. What on earth is He up to? The explanation is that He is building quite a different house from the one you thought of—throwing out a new wing here, putting on an extra floor there, running up towers, making courtyards. You thought you were being made into a decent little cottage: but He is building a palace. He intends to come and live in it Himself."

—C. S. Lewis, *Mere Christianity*

Part 2 Video (15 min.)

Author and therapist Georgia Shaffer shares how God desires to lead us from anger to acceptance—and even acceptance in the midst of our anger.

Reflection Questions

1. Where have you already given yourself "permission to grieve"? As a result, what healing or change have you seen so far?

2. What do you think of Georgia's statement, "Anger is a good feeling"? How have you been dealing with your anger, in both healthy and unhealthy ways?

3. "If you want to grow through the experience, you have to grow through the pain." Where haven't you "done the emotional work" yet? Why those areas, in particular? How can you begin to open these areas to God's healing?

4. What was the most important thing to you in this session?

Acceptance Action Steps

*How can you take what you've learned today and make it real in your life? Review and choose one or more of the options below— or if God is prompting you to do something else, do **that**!*

- **Eliminate old "memory pegs."** There will always be memories, places, and thoughts that will remind you of your past life. Minimize them. Stay away from old hangouts; don't listen to old songs that remind you of your past—for now. In time, those things may be okay to reintroduce—or maybe they'll no longer hold any attraction for you. But give yourself space to heal.

- **Begin creating new memories.** Purposely do new things with your friends or your kids that will create new memories. Take a trip or plan a special meal together. Take photos of your activities, and then post them around your house to remind you of your new life.

- **Stop "medicating" the pain.** Are you medicating on shopping, alcohol, men, food, or other distractions to keep you from facing the reality of your life? Identify your distractions or addictions, and then eliminate them. Ask someone to help you work through these issues. Be willing to be open and honest with that person (but don't turn her into another "medication"). The sooner you face your pain and work through it, the sooner you can accept your new life, and the faster your healing process will be.

- **Name your worries—and pray through them.** Are you ready to let go of "good enough," and embrace God's best? If not—or even if so—write out a list of those things you're worried about. When you're done writing, pray through your list. Give each one of those worries to God, and allow him to handle them the way he wants them handled. If you like, tear up your list when you're done, as a symbol of trusting God's work in your life.

Prayer of Acceptance

*Lord, help me to entrust you with those things that are
unjust, unacceptable, and painful beyond words. Help me
to surrender every broken piece of my house to you. Help
me to let go of what I cannot change, so that I can begin
the process of building a future. Help me to know what
boundaries to set up, and give me the strength to implement
them. Help me to surrender myself to the process of you
rebuilding what is broken, what is failed, what is lost, what
is imperfect, and to open up my heart to acceptance and
forgiveness. Bring people around me and to me, people who
can accept me and love me unconditionally as you make me
into the person you desire me to be. I entrust all I am and all
I have to you. In Jesus' name, amen.*

Prayer Requests

_____

_____

_____

_____

_____

_____

_____

_____

_____

_____

_____

_____

_____

Scripture Promises

The Lord is near to those who have a broken heart, and saves such as have a contrite spirit.
—Psalm 34:18

Yea, though I walk through the valley of the shadow of death, I will fear no evil; for You are with me; Your rod and Your staff, they comfort me.
—Psalm 23:4

Be anxious for nothing, but in everything by prayer and supplication, with thanksgiving, let your requests be made known to God; and the peace of God, which surpasses all understanding, will guard your hearts and minds through Christ Jesus.
—Philippians 4:6–7

Wait on the Lord; be of good courage, and He shall strengthen your heart; wait, I say, on the Lord!
—Psalm 27:14

But those who wait on the Lord shall renew their strength; they shall mount up with wings like eagles, they shall run and not be weary, they shall walk and not faint.
—Isaiah 40:31

[Cast] all your care upon Him, for He cares for you.
—1 Peter 5:7

He heals the brokenhearted and binds up their wounds.
—Psalm 147:3

Fear not, for I am with you; be not dismayed, for I am your God. I will strengthen you, yes, I will help you, I will uphold you with My righteous right hand.
—Isaiah 41:10

My soul, wait silently for God alone, for my expectation is from Him. He only is my rock and my salvation; He is my defense; I shall not be moved. In God is my salvation and my glory; the rock of my strength, and my refuge, is in God. Trust in Him at all times, you people; pour out your heart before Him; God is a refuge for us.
—Psalm 62:5–8

Cast your burden on the Lord, and He shall sustain you; He shall never permit the righteous to be moved.
—Psalm 55:22

Notes:

_____

_____

_____

_____

_____

_____

_____

_____

_____

_____

_____

_____

_____

_____

_____

_____

_____

_____

_____

_____

_____

_____

_____

Notes:

_____

_____

_____

_____

_____

_____

_____

_____

_____

_____

_____

_____

_____

_____

_____

_____

_____

_____

_____

_____

_____

_____

_____

_____

_____

_____

_____

Forgiveness

In this session, we will discuss one of the most difficult things women of divorce struggle with—not only forgiving the other person or persons, but also ourselves.

> *"For if you forgive other people when they sin against you, your heavenly Father will also forgive you. But if you do not forgive others their sins, your Father will not forgive your sins."*
>
> —*Matthew 6:14–15 (NIV)*

It's been said that not forgiving another person is like drinking poison and hoping the other person dies. Refusing to forgive is a never-ending battle that leads to bitterness, and keeps you in bondage to anger and resentment. Yet no matter who you are, when injustices have been done or false accusations have been made, it takes everything in you and God's supernatural power and love to help you walk out the act of forgiveness.

—*Michelle Borquez*

*P*art 1 *V*ideo   (20 min.)

Jo Ann Aleman shares about the importance of forgiveness in her own healing.

*D*iscussion *Q*uestions

As you're willing, share your answers to the following questions:

1. Why is it so hard to forgive? What are the consequences of not forgiving—for us, for those around us, and for those we need to forgive?

2. How have you learned to forgive yourself during this process? Why is receiving God's forgiveness for our own actions so important?

3. What's the difference between forgiveness and trust? Share an example, if you can.

4. Does forgiveness mean we have to be friends with the other person? Does it mean we have to trust them ever again? Why or why not?

no, no

5. Why is blaming others so damaging to our lives?

Part 2 Video (20 min.)

Paige Henderson shares insights on what forgiveness means and what it does not mean.

Reflection Questions

1. What "nasty little cousins" have come along with the bitterness or unforgiveness you've harbored? How have they negatively affected other areas of your life?

2. Do you really believe that God loves and forgives you? Why? How is the answer you just gave affecting your own ability to forgive others right now?

3. What's the difference between forgiveness and reconciliation? How did Paige's explanation help you better understand this difference?

4. Regarding this issue of forgiveness, where do you most need to trust God right now?

"*To love* means loving the unlovable. To forgive means pardoning the unpardonable. Faith means believing the unbelievable. Hope means hoping when everything seems hopeless."

—*G. K. Chesterton*

Forgiveness Action Steps

How do you need to make forgiveness a bigger part of your life this week? Review and choose one or more of the options below—or if God is prompting you to do something else, do that!

- **Choose to forgive.** Where do you need to make that choice this week? Does it involve specific actions by your ex-spouse or others, or are you at the point where you're saying, "I have to let it all go or it'll drag me down with it"? Respond to the Spirit's direction, and commit to forgiving the people and actions—no matter how many times the hurt comes back up.

- **Take your thoughts captive (2 Corinthians 10:5).** What thoughts or emotions seem to be controlling your life right now? Resolve not to give them that power over you. Consciously address those thoughts and emotions this week; turn each of them over to God as you notice them popping up.

- **Choose to accept God's forgiveness to you.** Acknowledge how you've failed God. Avoid playing the blame game—or the desire to add "but he/she . . ." to your confession before God. Accept your own role and your own reactions in what's occurred. Then, ask God's forgiveness and express your desire to walk in obedience. Spend some extra time in this week's Scripture Promises, as well, to gain a deeper sense of God's forgiveness toward you—and the need to forgive others.

- **Ask your children's forgiveness.** How has bitterness affected your actions toward your children—and thus affected their hearts? Drain that poison now. Ask your children's forgiveness for things you may have said and done toward them in anger and bitterness—as well as things you've said and done toward your ex-spouse in front of them. Help them to heal as well, even as you engage in your own journey of healing.

Prayer of Forgiveness

*Lord, you know those to whom I still hold bitterness
and unforgiveness—those toward whom I am angry and
resentful. You know and see all the bad thoughts, vengeful
motives, and angry attitudes that lie in the dark places of
my soul. Help me to release these things to you, and move
ahead into the purposes you have for my life. Give me the
strength and wisdom to do what I don't feel capable of
doing. I exchange my heart today for your heart of love and
forgiveness, and I will stand in faith, knowing you are for
me. In Jesus' name, amen.*

Prayer Requests

_____

_____

_____

_____

_____

_____

_____

_____

_____

_____

_____

_____

_____

_____

_____

_____

Scripture Promises

Therefore, as the elect of God, holy and beloved, put on tender mercies, kindness, humility, meekness, longsuffering; bearing with one another, and forgiving one another, if anyone has a complaint against another; even as Christ forgave you, so you also must do.
—Colossians 3:12–13

If we confess our sins, He is faithful and just to forgive us our sins and to cleanse us from all unrighteousness.
—1 John 1:9

The Lord is merciful and gracious, slow to anger, and abounding in mercy. He will not always strive with us, nor will He keep His anger forever. He has not dealt with us according to our sins, nor punished us according to our iniquities. For as the heavens are high above the earth, so great is His mercy toward those who fear Him; as far as the east is from the west, so far has He removed our transgressions from us.
—Psalm 103:8–12

Who is a God like You, pardoning iniquity and passing over the transgression of the remnant of His heritage? He does not retain His anger forever, because He delights in mercy.
—Micah 7:18

Let all bitterness, wrath, anger, clamor, and evil speaking be put away from you, with all malice. And be kind to one another, tenderhearted, forgiving one another, even as God in Christ forgave you.
—Ephesians 4:31–32

Do not repay anyone evil for evil. Be careful to do what is right in the eyes of everyone. If it is possible, as far as it depends on you, live at peace with everyone. Do not take revenge, my dear friends, but leave room for God's wrath, for it is written: "It is mine to avenge; I will repay," says the Lord.
—Romans 12:17–19 (NIV)

Be angry, and do not sin": do not let the sun go down on your wrath.
—Ephesians 4:26

Hatred stirs up strife, but love covers all sins.
—Proverbs 10:12

My dear brothers and sisters, take note of this: Everyone should be quick to listen, slow to speak and slow to become angry.
—James 1:19 (NIV)

Notes:

The Loneliness Giant

In this session, we will discuss and identify practical ways to cope with feelings of loneliness.

> *Be strong and of good courage, do not fear nor be afraid of them; for the Lord your God, He is the One who goes with you. He will not leave you nor forsake you.*
>
> —*Deuteronomy 31:6*

The agony of being alone, the nights when you're all alone and the kids are in bed, it's just you and the quiet— and the feelings of loneliness sweep in and surround you. Moments like these are some of the hardest. In the busyness of the day it is easy to forget the pain and loss. But when nighttime falls, or when the kids are with their dad, there's no one but you. It's almost unbearable. And then there are the "loneliness reminders" to remind you that you're divorced: sitting alone at church, or sitting alone at dinner, or sitting alone at home when everyone else is out enjoying themselves. The first year it can even be difficult to get out of your pajamas and get the kids to school on time.

—*Michelle Borquez*

Part 1 Video (20 min.)

Gretchen Goldsmith, a women's ministry leader with many years' experience leading divorce recovery groups, shares about her own struggles with—and victories over—loneliness.

Discussion Questions

Discuss the following questions with your group:

1. When do you most often experience, as Gretchen puts it, "loneliness tsunamis"?

2. What mistakes are you most vulnerable to when loneliness hits? What do you expect to get out of those behaviors? What do you end up getting out of them instead?

3. Where do you think God is in your loneliness? What truths from Scripture do you hang on to when you're lonely?

4. How easy or difficult is it for you to accept loneliness as part of the grieving process?

5. Toward the end of this segment, Gretchen talks about seeking out healthy relationships with more mature women. Do you have any of those right now? How can—or could—they help you to deal with loneliness, and with the healing process?

Part 2 Video (20 min.)

Sharon Kay Ball brings insights from both sides of the therapist's couch on how to get through the challenges of loneliness.

Reflection Questions

1. What do you find yourself still reaching out for that's no longer there? What is it you miss most about those things?

2. What "harsh" thoughts come to mind when you're alone? What are some healthy ways you can be kind to yourself, to help replace those harsh thoughts? What healthy activities are you now free to try?

3. How can being alone be an opportunity to rediscover yourself? What might that look like for you, personally?

4. Who are the safe people in your life who you can open up to and, in turn, grant them permission to reach out to you?

5. What would you like to tell God about the loneliness you're experiencing? (If you're alone, stop what you're doing and tell God right now.)

Loneliness Action Steps

How are you dealing with your loneliness right now? And how can you take what you've discussed today and use it so that you can start becoming whole again? Review and choose one or more of the options below—or if God is prompting you to do something else, do that!

- **Reach out to God.** Instead of spending time on the phone or computer when the "loneliness tsunami" hits, reach out for your Bible. Listen to worship songs. Read the biography of a great Christian who has been through struggles, such as *The Hiding Place* by Corrie ten Boom, or any of the Christian Heroes Series by Janet Benge. Spend time praying. You'll be amazed at how it will change your heart and how much less alone you'll feel.

- **Think about others instead of yourself.** Donate your time and talent to a cause or church. There is nothing more healing than helping those who are in worse condition than yourself—and there's many more of those people than you may think. Just like you, they need the help more than they're willing to admit. So start reaching out.

- **Connect with other Christian women.** Find safe people who will understand and empathize with you rather than condemn or judge you—or "enable" you. Find women who will speak the truth in love to you—and be ready to receive both the truth and the love. Often the safest people are women who've walked in your shoes.

- **Discover a new activity.** What have you always wanted to try? Now's the time. Take an art or cooking class, learn an instrument—or maybe like Michelle, get into rock climbing. On days your kids are gone or on the weekends, have a plan in place so you don't find yourself totally free with too much time to think and feel sorry for yourself.

- **Begin doing activities alone.** Yes, it will feel uncomfortable at first, but begin seeing this as something positive. Start with activities where a lot of other people are involved, like seeing a movie or sitting in a crowded coffee shop, reading a book. Get to the place where you can be comfortable with being alone.

Prayer for Loneliness

Lord, in my moments of loneliness, when I feel abandoned and lost, fill my heart with the assurance of your presence. Help me to remember your loving promises of strength when I feel weak, and peace when I feel fear. Help me build friendships with others who have found you to be their Rock and their Fortress. Keep my heart, body, mind, and spirit in right relationship with you so I can continue to become whole and truly live again. In Jesus' name, amen.

Prayer Requests

_____

_____

_____

_____

_____

_____

_____

_____

_____

_____

_____

_____

_____

_____

_____

_____

Scripture Promises

*Let your conduct be without covetousness; be content
with such things as you have. For He Himself has
said, "I will never leave you nor forsake you."*
—Hebrews 13:5

*"My grace is sufficient for you, for my power is made
perfect in weakness." Therefore I will boast all the more gladly
about my weaknesses, so that Christ's power may rest on me.*
—2 Corinthians 12:9 (NIV)

*The Lord your God in your midst, the Mighty One, will
save; He will rejoice over you with gladness. He will quiet
you with His love, He will rejoice over you with singing.*
—Zephaniah 3:17

*The Lord is near to those who have a broken
heart, and saves such as have a contrite spirit.*
—Psalm 34:18

*Nevertheless I am continually with You; You
hold me by my right hand. You will guide me with
Your counsel, and afterward receive me to glory.*
—Psalm 73:23–24

Therefore I say to you, do not worry about your life, what you will eat; nor about the body, what you will put on. . . . And do not seek what you should eat or what you should drink, nor have an anxious mind. For all these things the nations of the world seek after, and your Father knows that you need these things. But seek the kingdom of God, and all these things shall be added to you.
—Luke 12:22, 29–31

For I am persuaded that neither death nor life, nor angels nor principalities nor powers, nor things present nor things to come, nor height nor depth, nor any other created thing, shall be able to separate us from the love of God which is in Christ Jesus our Lord.
—Romans 8:38–39

Notes:

_____

_____

_____

_____

_____

_____

_____

_____

_____

_____

_____

_____

_____

_____

_____

_____

_____

_____

_____

_____

_____

_____

_____

_____

_____

_____

_____

_____

_____

_____

The Real Enemy: Lies Women Believe

In this session, we will discuss the negative thoughts and other lies we believe, like the lie that says God no longer loves us. We will examine where those lies really come from, and how to stand firm against them—knowing we have value in the eyes of God.

> *"No weapon formed against you shall prosper, and every tongue which rises against you in judgment you shall condemn. This is the heritage of the servants of the Lord, and their righteousness is from Me," says the Lord.*
>
> —Isaiah 54:17

"You're not worthy." "No one will ever want you." "Look how low you've fallen." "What reason do you have to live?" Do these lies sound familiar to you? Many women have to fight these messages every day and resist the enemy and his plan to destroy them. Who is our real enemy? Is it our ex-husband? Do we feel God is against us?

—*Michelle Borquez*

Part 1 Video (15 min.)

Author and counselor Georgia Shaffer discusses with Michelle how to use God's truth to counter the lies that women believe about themselves.

Discussion Questions

As you're willing, share your answers to the following questions:

1. Georgia shared about the many things she had lost in the wake of her divorce. What other things has the enemy taken from you, in addition to your marriage?

   – cofidence
   – security
   – future as I knew it

2. What lies do you believe about yourself when you're feeling vulnerable? How well do you recognize them as lies? Explain.

   – unlovable
   – unattractive

3. How do you deal with the fear that life will never get better? What "little things" do (or can) help you heal?

- pray
- meet w/ friends
- treat myself

4. What things do you still have? How can focusing on those things, instead of on what you've lost, give you hope and strength?

- my children
- my idenity
- my pride

*P*art 2 *V*ideo (20 min.)

Dr. Tim Alan Gardner helps us identify and take a stand against the real enemy in our lives.

*R*eflection *Q*uestions

1. Who or what do you think of as your enemies at this point in your journey? How can you see the real enemy using these people or things against you?

2. All of us need to take time to honestly evaluate why the marriage failed. What part was your responsibility? Which part was not yours? What have you learned?

- put kids first
- didn't help to nurture continuously
- not mine - affair
    - lack of trust & attention

- God
- Space
- kids

3. What is God teaching you about his mercy and grace when you fail?

    — He loves me no matter what!
    — He has great plans for me

4. Where do you still have problems believing that God loves you and wants his best for you? How can you take hold of his promises to you?

    Jeremiah 29:11

> " Is *society* dragging you in the opposite direction
> from where Jesus calls you? Then acknowledge that
> your life is part of a spiritual war between God and
> Satan, declare your side, and get on with it."
>
> —George Barna, *Revolution*

God's Truth Action Steps

How can you take what you've learned today and make it real in your life? Review and choose one or more of the options below—or if God is prompting you to do something else, do that!

- **Respond in the Spirit instead of the flesh.** For example, if your ex-husband does something that presses on a place of woundedness in your heart, remember that it's the enemy using him to try to keep you distracted on your path to healing and wholeness. Don't react. Instead, take time, breathe, and ask the Lord for a heart of love and wisdom in that situation, and then ask him to help you respond in kindness.

- **Identify and release your "victim mentality."** Where specifically do you believe the enemy's lies about you—and thus reject God's truth? Where are you most focused on yourself—and what you can (or can't) do? Choose to believe God's truth and in God's love for you. Choose to live in dependence on him. In time, you will move from being a victim to a victor in Christ.

- **Replace the enemy's lies with God's truth.** Spend extra time in this week's Scripture Promises, and in God's Word in general. Also consider finding a Bible resource that specifically focuses on God's promises for you, such as "Bible Promises for Hope and Courage" (Rose Publishing). Read what God has to say about you, and make the decision to believe it.

Prayer Against the Enemy

Lord, help me to recognize the enemy's work in my life. Open my eyes to the way he comes to steal from me, destroy me, and ultimately tempt me to things that are not life-giving. Help me to see those judgmental accusations and put-downs as lies of the enemy, and help me to embrace your promises instead. In moments when I feel unlovable, help me remember that there is no condemnation for those who are in Christ. Lord, in moments I feel weak, be my strength. In moments I feel defeated, rise up in me and help me stand against the weapons the enemy wants to use to destroy me. Keep me rooted in your truth, not lies. You are my everything, and all I desire. In Jesus' name, amen.

Prayer Requests

_____

_____

_____

_____

_____

_____

_____

_____

_____

_____

_____

_____

_____

_____

_____

_____

Scripture Promises

For God did not send His Son into the world to condemn
the world, but that the world through Him might be saved.
—John 3:17

There is therefore now no condemnation to those
who are in Christ Jesus, who do not walk according
to the flesh, but according to the Spirit.
—Romans 8:1

"God resists the proud, but gives grace to the humble."
Therefore submit to God. Resist the devil and he will flee from
you. Draw near to God and He will draw near to you.
—James 4:6–8

Be alert and of sober mind. Your enemy the devil prowls around like a roaring lion looking for someone to devour. Resist him, standing firm in the faith, because you know that the family of believers throughout the world is undergoing the same kind of sufferings.
—1 Peter 5:8–9 (NIV)

Finally, be strong in the Lord and in his mighty power. Put on the full armor of God, so that you can take your stand against the devil's schemes. For our struggle is not against flesh and blood, but against the rulers, against the authorities, against the powers of this dark world and against the spiritual forces of evil in the heavenly realms. . . . And pray in the Spirit on all occasions with all kinds of prayers and requests. With this in mind, be alert and always keep on praying for all the Lord's people.
—Ephesians 6:10–12, 18 (NIV)

Notes:

Respect Yourself

In this session, we will learn ways to recover self-respect and find our identity in God.

> *You also, as living stones, are being built up a spiritual house, a holy priesthood, to offer up spiritual sacrifices acceptable to God through Jesus Christ.*
>
> —1 Peter 2:5

It's not easy to respect yourself, or feel worthy of respect, when you are at one of the lowest moments of your life. Your world has been shattered into a million little pieces and your value has been crushed by the horrible outcome of divorce. We tend to attract people at our common level of woundedness—or our level of health. During this vulnerable time, we need to learn how to better care for ourselves and protect ourselves from predators and bad choices.

—*Michelle Borquez*

Part 1 Video (20 min.)

Tabitha Warren shares ways lack of self-respect led to poor choices as she rebuilt her life after divorce.

Discussion Questions (20 min.)

Share your answers to the following questions:

1. Where specifically do you struggle with self-respect, or with being overly focused on people-pleasing?

2. How do you usually respond to people who treat you with disrespect? Why is it so hard to put up good boundaries?

3. Which of the lies Tabitha mentioned resonated most with you—or is there another she didn't mention? Why does that one hit so hard?

4. How does forgiveness lead to self-respect? What's the difference between forgiving and excusing?

5. What was the most important part of Tabitha's testimony for you? Why?

*P*art 2 *V*ideo (20 min.)

Leslie Vernick talks about emotionally destructive relationships and ways to become emotionally healthy.

*R*eflection *Q*uestions

1. When women go through the devastation of divorce, it's easy to make bad dating decisions. What are the red flags to watch for when you start dating?

2. What are some practical ways that can you evaluate a person's character?

3. Why is it better to say "no" early in a dating relationship—or in any relationship with a man? Share a personal example, if you're willing.

4. How can you find the balance between trust and caution?

5. Are you, or have you recently been, in an emotionally destructive relationship? Who are the safe people you can share with to gain wisdom, protection, and/or healing?

Respect Action Steps

How can you begin believing God's words about you, and walk that out in your life? Review and choose one or more of the options below—or if God is prompting you to do something else, do that!

- **Understand God's love for you, and start believing it.** Think of some key Scriptures you can dwell on daily. Start with this week's Scripture Promises, and go from there. In addition, start sharing God's truth about you with others; there's a good chance that they need to hear God's promises, too.

- **Treat yourself as God treats you.** How does knowing how God sees you, and loves you, enable you to respect yourself more? Write down a few ways you need to better respect yourself in relationships—including those with your former spouse and in your own thought life—and begin acting on them. Expect the enemy's lies to ramp up as you put this into practice, and commit to countering the enemy's lies with God's words about you.

- **Learn to say "no."** Where are you allowing the men in your life to cross your boundaries, whether you're in a relationship with them or not? And where is that line? Establish your boundaries, and keep to them. Show yourself some respect. In the process, you'll learn about these men's true characters—if they respect you back, they'll honor you and those boundaries.

Respect Prayer

Lord, forgive me for not loving myself as you love me. Help me to believe deep inside that I am your beloved child and the apple of your eye. Give me the strength to stand up in my relationships—especially in the areas where I haven't respected myself. Help me to think about things that will encourage my heart, mind, and spirit, instead of things that will bring death to my soul. Give me wisdom to recognize people who are not safe and don't care about me the way you do, and give me the strength to walk away from them. In Jesus' name, amen.

Prayer Requests

_____

_____

_____

_____

_____

_____

_____

_____

_____

_____

_____

_____

_____

_____

_____

_____

Scripture Promises

But as many as received Him, to them He gave the right to become children of God, to those who believe in His name.
—John 1:12

But now, O Lord, You are our Father; we are the clay, and You our potter; and all we are the work of Your hand.
—Isaiah 64:8

For I know the thoughts that I think toward you, says the Lord, thoughts of peace and not of evil, to give you a future and a hope.
—Jeremiah 29:11

Do not be anxious about anything, but in every situation, by prayer and petition, with thanksgiving, present your requests to God. And the peace of God, which transcends all understanding, will guard your hearts and your minds in Christ Jesus. Finally, brothers and sisters, whatever is true, whatever is noble, whatever is right, whatever is pure, whatever is lovely, whatever is admirable—if anything is excellent or praiseworthy—think about such things.
—Philippians 4:6–8 (NIV)

And not only that, but we also glory in tribulations, knowing that tribulation produces perseverance; and perseverance, character; and character, hope. Now hope does not disappoint, because the love of God has been poured out in our hearts by the Holy Spirit who was given to us.
—Romans 5:3–5

Commit your way to the Lord, trust also in Him, and He shall bring it to pass. He shall bring forth your righteousness as the light, and your justice as the noonday.
—Psalm 37:5–6

Who shall separate us from the love of Christ? Shall tribulation, or distress . . .? Yet in all these things we are more than conquerors through Him who loved us. For I am persuaded that neither death nor life, nor angels nor principalities nor powers, nor things present nor things to come, nor height nor depth, nor any other created thing, shall be able to separate us from the love of God which is in Christ Jesus our Lord.
—Romans 8:35, 37–39

Notes:

_____
_____
_____
_____
_____
_____
_____
_____
_____
_____
_____
_____
_____
_____
_____
_____
_____
_____
_____
_____
_____
_____
_____
_____
_____
_____

Sexless and Single: Sex and Dating

In this session, we will discuss sexuality and wholeness, following God's good plan for sexuality within the covenant relationship of marriage. We will learn to exercise a spirit of wisdom and restoration rather than of judgment and self-condemnation.

> *For you were bought at a price; therefore glorify God in your body and in your spirit, which are God's.*
>
> —*1 Corinthians 6:20*

We all need to be loved. And we all desire closeness, to feel truly cherished. Our brains are hardwired from birth to need intimacy. But are we really getting the love and commitment we crave when we join ourselves with someone who is not our spouse? These principles apply to us just as much as they apply to our teenagers.

—*Michelle Borquez*

$\mathcal{P}art\ 1\ \mathcal{V}ideo$ (20 min.)

Dr. Tim Alan Gardner gives tips on making good choices with and about men—and for ourselves.

$\mathcal{D}iscussion\ \mathcal{Q}uestions$

Share your answers to the following questions:

1. Sexual needs are good and God-given. We all need love and affirmation, but do we really get that when we join ourselves with someone who isn't our spouse?

2. Dr. Gardner says that if a man walks away because you won't have sex with him, "Good riddance." How do you balance the rejection with the desire for closeness?

   it hurts but he doesn't value you.

3. What do we do with our deep desire for sexual expression and emotional intimacy so that we don't—as Michelle puts it—give pieces of ourselves away?

4. What's your biggest takeaway from what Dr. Gardner shared?

"*[T]hose* who indulge in [sex outside marriage] are trying to isolate one kind of union (the sexual) from all the other kinds of union which were intended to go along with it and make up the total union."

—C. S. Lewis

*P*art 2 *V*ideo (15 min.)

Dr. Catherine Hart Weber shows how our drive for connection and intimacy can bring true satisfaction and wholeness.

*R*eflection *Q*uestions

1. Sexuality is good and God-given, but often it is misused. Sometimes women give sex in order to get closeness. What mistakes do women make when dating?

2. What does sex mean to you? What do you get out of it, or have you gotten out of it in the past?

3. How can you find closeness and intimacy in positive ways, other than engaging in sex or relationships you're not yet ready for?

   Share verbally details of your life

4. Where do you need God's wholeness, healing, and wisdom when it comes to your current relationships or behaviors with men? How can you get the help you need with it?

Relationship Action Steps

How can you take what you've learned today and make it real in your life? Review and choose one or more of the options below—or if God is prompting you to do something else, do that!

- **Develop "normal" guy friendships.** Learn to develop relationships with men that aren't intended to lead to dating or sex. Learn to maintain your boundaries around "safe" guys; they will respect you more for it. In addition, such relationships will help you keep your head on straight—"I don't have to have that kind of relationship with a man"—and help you avoid the trap of seduction.

- **Let men pursue you.** Hear us correctly: This advice isn't sexual, nor is it about "playing hard to get"—it's about respecting yourself enough to not act needy. If you're in a dating relationship—or especially if you're not—don't call, email, or text him all the time. Smothering a man sends the message that you're not strong; in addition, some men (particularly, the worst ones) will detect weakness as an opportunity for taking advantage of you sexually or otherwise.

- **Learn to depend on the perfect man—Jesus Christ.** Don't ever rely on your own strength. Become totally dependent on Christ. In our own strength we are completely weak, especially when we're in as vulnerable a place as being divorced. When you're feeling vulnerable or in need of intimacy, don't turn to substitutes; turn to the One who can bring you peace in the middle of your struggles to feel valued and loved.

*P*rayer for *R*elationships

*Lord, help me to keep my heart and eyes focused on you,
and on all you desire for my life. Give me strength to follow
your principles in moments of temptation. Lord, I know your
forgiveness is always available to me even when I sin, but I
desire to honor you and myself with my actions. Continue
to show me ways to protect my heart, body, mind, and soul
and to not medicate on counterfeits that will leave me empty.
Thank you for your love. In Jesus' name, amen.*

*P*rayer *R*equests

_____
_____
_____
_____
_____
_____
_____
_____
_____
_____
_____
_____
_____
_____
_____
_____

Scripture Promises

He has sent Me to heal the brokenhearted, to proclaim liberty to the captives, and the opening of the prison to those who are bound . . . to comfort all who mourn . . . to give them beauty for ashes, the oil of joy for mourning.
—Isaiah 61:1–3

Yes, I have loved you with an everlasting love; therefore with lovingkindness I have drawn you.
—Jeremiah 31:3

For it is said, "The two will become one flesh." But whoever is united with the Lord is one with him in spirit. Flee from sexual immorality. All other sins a person commits are outside the body, but whoever sins sexually, sins against their own body. Do you not know that your bodies are temples of the Holy Spirit, who is in you, whom you have received from God? You are not your own.
—1 Corinthians 6:16–18 (NIV)

For this is the will of God, your sanctification: that you should abstain from sexual immorality; that each of you should know how to possess his own vessel in sanctification and honor. ...For God did not call us to uncleanness, but in holiness.
—1 Thessalonians 4:3–4, 7

The Lord upholds all who fall, and raises up all who are bowed down.
—Psalm 145:14

Trust in the Lord with all your heart, and lean not on your own understanding; in all your ways, acknowledge Him, and He shall direct your paths.
—Proverbs 3:5–6

*N*otes:

_____

_____

_____

_____

_____

_____

_____

_____

_____

_____

_____

_____

_____

_____

_____

_____

_____

_____

_____

_____

_____

_____

_____

_____

_____

Notes:

_____

_____

_____

_____

_____

_____

_____

_____

_____

_____

_____

_____

_____

_____

_____

_____

_____

_____

_____

_____

_____

_____

_____

_____

_____

_____

_____

_____

Beyond the Shame and Guilt

In this session, we will discuss how to move forward on the path from shame and guilt to joy and confidence in the Lord.

> *The Lord is merciful and gracious, slow to anger, and abounding in mercy. He will not always strive with us, nor will He keep His anger forever. He has not dealt with us according to our sins, nor punished us according to our iniquities.*
>
> —Psalm 103:8–10

Shame and guilt go hand in hand with divorce. It's almost impossible to not feel like there's a big "D" for Divorce on your forehead and a black cloud following your every move. This is something all of us naturally feel at first. But to stay in bondage to shame and to continue to be enslaved by the guilt will not only keep you from your purpose but will also keep you distant in your relationship with God. If you don't feel worthy enough, good enough, or clean enough, you most likely don't feel you can approach the Lord. Yet his mercies, forgiveness, and grace are awaiting you today.

—*Michelle Borquez*

$\mathcal{P}$art 1 $\mathcal{V}$ideo (20 min.)

Sharon Kay Ball shares her struggle against the lies that shame wants us to believe.

$\mathcal{D}$iscussion $\mathcal{Q}$uestions

Share your answers to the following questions:

1. What burdens of guilt and shame do you carry from your divorce? From your past? How do the two feed each other?

2. How do we deal with the failure in our marriages, perhaps even our lives? How do we accept the responsibility for our own actions without blaming ourselves for other people's choices?

3. What lies has the enemy been feeding you, which in turn further feed your shame and guilt? How can you counter those lies?

4. Where are "the little rays of light and hope" right now, in this season of your life? How can you more actively pursue that hope?

Part 2 Video (20 min.)

Dale Dunnewold talks about ways to combat the lies about our worthlessness by finding our true worth and identity in Christ.

Reflection Questions

1. Shame is a lie that says, "There's something wrong with me. I am so messed up that God can never love me, and neither can anyone else." How has your divorce contributed to this lie?

2. What false expectations or beliefs did you bring into your marriage? What were you really saying or thinking through those assumptions? How do they relate to your shame?

3. What things are you scared to "show" God (even though he already sees it)—or to let God show you? Why?

4. Why do you know that shame is a lie? How can you remind yourself of the truth of God's love and acceptance toward you?

5. What was your biggest takeaway from this session? What do you think God wants you to do about it?

Rejecting Shame Action Steps

How can you begin moving from shame and guilt and into hope?
Review and choose one or more of the options below—or if God is
prompting you to do something else, do that!

- **Accept how God sees you.** No matter what you have done,
no matter how much destruction your choices have caused,
God is willing to forgive you. Put away the lie that says you
cannot be forgiven and embrace the truth that Jesus truly
loves you and forgives you. Spend some extra time in the
Scripture Promises; focus on what God thinks of you rather
than on what people think of you (or what you think they
think). Give yourself grace; know that you don't have to be
perfect, but look to Jesus to perfect you daily.

- **Bury your past—literally.** Write down any shame and guilt
you still may be struggling to let go; determine to let these
things die. Pray to God to give you the ability to let those
things go, and then bury the paper(s) in the ground (or burn
it, throw it away—whatever works best for you). Thank God
for your past—because it's made you who you are today—but
let it die so that your future can live. You are forgiven: Now
go out with your head held high.

- **Help others.** There are people all around you going through
crises of some sort right now, so avoid the temptation to
self-pity and find someone else you can help. It doesn't have
to be someone going through a divorce or something you've
personally struggled with; at the same time, it's possible
that God wants to use your experiences to speak to others
who really need to hear it right now—people who need to
overcome their own shame and guilt. Let God lead you to the
right people, and serve them.

- **Pursue hope.** Reflect again on those "little rays of light and
hope" that you've experienced recently, and consider ways
you can actively pursue that hope. What things do you look
forward to in this season of your life, and how can you make
those things your focus, instead of the shameful and painful
things of your past? Commit to developing the hope that's in
you, and to sharing it with others as well.

Rejecting Shame Prayer

Lord, I have not liked myself for so long. I have harbored this shame and guilt, and need your help to let it go. Give me your supernatural strength to be able to let go of my past. Allow me to be convicted by it as you still need to work in me, but deliver me from condemnation from the enemy, others, and myself. Help me to walk in the freedom of knowing that you love me just as I am, not because of what I've done or haven't done. I love you, and my desire is to please you out of this love. Help me to walk in the freedom of knowing that even when I make mistakes, you are there to lift me up and help me live again with hope and purpose for the future. In Jesus' name, amen.

Prayer Requests

_____

_____

_____

_____

_____

_____

_____

_____

_____

_____

_____

_____

_____

_____

Scripture Promises

Therefore, if anyone is in Christ, he is a new creation; old things have passed away; behold, all things have become new. . . . For He made Him who knew no sin to be sin for us, that we might become the righteousness of God in Him.
—2 Corinthians 5:17, 21

Why are you cast down, O my soul? And why are you disquieted within me? Hope in God; for I shall yet praise Him, the help of my countenance and my God.
—Psalm 42:11

There is therefore now no condemnation to those who are in Christ Jesus, who do not walk according to the flesh, but according to the Spirit. For the law of the Spirit of life in Christ Jesus has made me free from the law of sin and death.
—Romans 8:1–2

The Lord is close to the brokenhearted and saves those who are crushed in spirit.
—Psalm 34:18 (NIV)

Let us draw near to God with a sincere heart and with the full assurance that faith brings, having our hearts sprinkled to cleanse us from a guilty conscience and having our bodies washed with pure water. Let us hold unswervingly to the hope we profess, for he who promised is faithful. And let us consider how we may spur one another on toward love and good deeds.
—Hebrews 10:22–24 (NIV)

Keep my soul, and deliver me; let me not be ashamed, for I put my trust in You. Let integrity and uprightness preserve me, for I wait for You.
—Psalm 25:20–21

If you confess with your mouth the Lord Jesus and believe in your heart that God has raised Him from the dead, you will be saved. . . . For the Scripture says, "Whoever believes on Him will not be put to shame."
—Romans 10:9, 11

*N*otes:

_____

_____

_____

_____

_____

_____

_____

_____

_____

_____

_____

_____

_____

_____

_____

_____

_____

_____

_____

_____

_____

_____

_____

_____

_____

_____

Discovering a Whole New You

In this session, we will discuss the next steps in our new lives, and how God can turn pain into new dreams for the future.

> But those who wait on the Lord shall renew their strength; they shall mount up with wings like eagles, they shall run and not be weary, they shall walk and not faint.
>
> —Isaiah 40:31

God is in the business of creating something wonderful out of the ashes. No matter how devastating your story, if you allow God to rebuild the pieces and show you who you are in Christ, you will laugh, you will love, and you definitely will live again.

—Michelle Borquez

$\mathcal{P}art\ 1\ \mathcal{V}ideo$ (20 min.)

Michelle leads a roundtable discussion exploring the journeys of four women who walked through the fire of divorce to find their lives renewed, and their value in Christ.

$\mathcal{D}iscussion\ \mathcal{Q}uestions$

Share your answers to the following questions:

1. How much do you believe that "God doesn't waste any of our pain"? What examples can you give to help support this statement?

2. Why is it so important to take the time to heal emotionally before dating again?

3. What losses are your children or other family members still processing? How have you helped them to process, even in the midst of your own recovery?

4. How close or distant does God feel at this point in your journey? How does what the women shared at the end of this segment speak to where you're at right now? Where can you see God's faithfulness, no matter what you're feeling?

Part 2 Video (20 min.)

Paige Henderson and Dale Dunnewold share insights for finding wholeness, acceptance, and completeness—in other words, a whole new you!

Reflection Questions

1. What things have already begun to help you feel whole again? What are some of the signs that you're already moving forward in the healing process?

2. In your own words, when will you know when you're ready to date again?

3. Why is it so easy to be restless, and look for satisfaction and peace in places other than God?

4. Where does God still need to heal you, when it comes to your ability to trust men (or people in general) again?

5. What do you think your next steps are in the healing process?

New Life Action Steps

So, what's next? How can you take what you've learned today—and throughout this season—and make it real in your life? Review and choose one or more of the options below—or if God is prompting you to do something else, do that!

- **Speak life to yourself.** We've focused a lot on countering the enemy's lies and replacing them with God's truth. Now, it's time to be not so focused on the enemy's lies (though still mindful of them). What does God have to say about you? What are the good plans you already know he has for you? Make those things your focus this week, and beyond. Regularly remind yourself of those things—and don't be shy about reminding God about them as well. Yes, he already knows, but he wants to partner with you in making them happen. Let God know you're "all in," and let him guide you deeper into the new life and purpose he has planned for you.

- **Try new things.** New things promote growth, and new life. So what would you like to try? It can be as immediately life-changing as a new career or new place to live, or as simple as a new activity, a new route to work, or a new look. Whatever you decide, enjoy it. Give yourself permission to experiment, and maybe even to fail, knowing that even those initial failures will open you up to a new direction you hadn't noticed before.

- **Create a mission statement.** Where do you want to go from here? What do you want your dating life, your spiritual life, your financial life, your family life, etc. to look like? What do you need to do to get there, and who can help you? Write it all down. You'll probably want to write down everything that comes to mind first, then boil it down to something simpler, and then create action steps for each area. Once you can see that plan, start making it happen!

Again, give yourself grace in this process. Things may not happen as quickly as you like—or God may have other plans that look different from yours. But as you trust God, and yourself, change will come. Don't forget to celebrate each change as it comes.

Prayer of New Life

*Lord, your word tells us that your plans for us are good—
plans to give us a future and hope. It's our desire to hope
and trust in you completely. Help the desires of our hearts to
line up with your perfect will for our lives. Give us wisdom
and discernment regarding work, relationships, finances,
and everything else that concerns us. Help us to be women
who walk in integrity and in the Spirit. We know we can do
all things with you and through you. Help us to walk in your
joy, knowing we've been created for your purpose. We pray
all this in the name of Jesus, amen.*

Prayer Requests

_____

_____

_____

_____

_____

_____

_____

_____

_____

_____

_____

_____

_____

_____

_____

_____

Scripture Promises

For I know the thoughts that I think toward you, says the
Lord, thoughts of peace and not of evil, to give you a future
and a hope. Then you will call upon Me and go and pray
to Me, and I will listen to you. And you will seek Me and
find Me, when you search for Me with all your heart.
—*Jeremiah 29:11–13*

And we know that all things work together
for good to those who love God, to those who
are the called according to His purpose.
—*Romans 8:28*

My Presence will go with you, and I will give you rest.
—*Exodus 33:14*

You are already clean because of the word I have spoken
to you. Remain in me, as I also remain in you. No branch
can bear fruit by itself; it must remain in the vine. Neither
can you bear fruit unless you remain in me. I am the vine;
you are the branches. If you remain in me and I in you, you
will bear much fruit; apart from me you can do nothing.
—*John 15:3–5 (NIV)*

God is our refuge and strength, a very present help in trouble. Therefore we will not fear. . . . "Be still, and know that I am God; I will be exalted among the nations, I will be exalted in the earth."
—Psalm 46:1–2, 10

Therefore, I urge you, brothers and sisters, in view of God's mercy, to offer your bodies as a living sacrifice, holy and pleasing to God—this is your true and proper worship. Do not conform to the pattern of this world, but be transformed by the renewing of your mind. Then you will be able to test and approve what God's will is—his good, pleasing and perfect will.
—Romans 12:1–2 (NIV)

Give attention to my words; incline your ear to my sayings. Do not let them depart from your eyes; keep them in the midst of your heart; for they are life to those who find them, and health to all their flesh. Keep your heart with all diligence, for out of it spring the issues of life.
—Proverbs 4:20–23

In all my prayers for all of you, I always pray with joy because of your partnership in the gospel from the first day until now, being confident of this, that he who began a good work in you will carry it on to completion until the day of Christ Jesus.
—Philippians 1:4–6

*N*otes:

_____

_____

_____

_____

_____

_____

_____

_____

_____

_____

_____

_____

_____

_____

_____

_____

_____

_____

_____

_____

_____

_____

_____

_____

_____

_____

*N*otes:

_____

_____

_____

_____

_____

_____

_____

_____

_____

_____

_____

_____

_____

_____

_____

_____

_____

_____

_____

_____

_____

_____

_____

_____

_____

_____

_____

Healing and Wholeness Start Here!

Sign up for the Live Again emails at
www.LiveAgainDVD.com/inspirations

Sign up for the Live Again discussion group at
LiveAgain-subscribe@yahoogroups.com

Share YOUR divorce recovery journey with the Live
Again Community. Send your video or your story to
your.stories@aspirepress.com

Hope for the Heart Biblical Counseling Library

The Freedom Series

When divorce devastates a home, or a woman experiences abuse, paralyzing fear, abandonment, rape, or abortion, she needs God's restoration and wholeness. The **Freedom Series** brings you true stories that show how to heal from the hurts, and experience joy again. These books are 96 pages, 4.5"x 6.5", Paperback.

ABUSE TO FAVOR
When abuse happens, as women we tend to take on the pain alone. But you aren't alone and you don't have to deal with it alone. This book helps women understand that it's not your fault and you don't have to face it alone. ISBN: 9781596366213

ABORTION TO MERCY
She never thought she would be in the situation of having an abortion and once it was over the pain was still there. But God has not abandoned you. This book helps you heal and move past the hurt. ISBN: 9781596366220

DIVORCE TO WHOLENESS
Divorce can tear you in half. It's not easy to deal with or sometimes even understand. With *Divorce to Wholeness* you learn how to put yourself back together and become whole again. ISBN: 9781596366237

FEAR TO COURAGE
Fear to Courage shows women that they don't have to be a slave to their fears and helps them truly define their fears and develop the courage to move past them. This book shows women that through Christ all things are possible. ISBN: 9781596366244

ABANDONMENT TO FORGIVENESS
At some point in every woman's life she has felt a sense of abandonment, for some this feeling is bigger than others. This book teaches women that no matter who has left you, God is always with you. ISBN: 9781596366251

DECEIVED TO DELIVERED
She never thought she would cross the line and have an affair, but she did. *Deceived to Delivered* shows women how to strengthen their boundaries and restore their relationships. ISBN: 9781596366268

8-Week Program
Live Again: Wholeness After Divorce
The only Christian divorce recovery program just for women

The Complete Kit contains:

- DVDs with all 8 sessions
- PDF files for promotional fliers, banners, posters, postcards, email header, and Facebook image
- One leader guide
- One participant guide with discussion questions
- One Live Again Journal
- Perfect to watch at home, for one-to-one mentoring or for groups of 2 or more